Some glass marbles
Tin lids
A pulley and some rope
Block of wood and wooden strips
A toy soldier
Some empty cotton reels
Two wooden skewers
A few nails
Soft wire
String and strong thread
Round cheese boxes
Corrugated cardboard
A playing card
A rubber ball
A toy balloon
A tube of glue
A toy lorry

Series 621

Do you know that you use a lever every time you press an electric light switch, turn a key in a lock, or dig the garden?

In this fascinating book you will also learn—with the help of simple, safe experiments—how pulleys are used to lift heavy weights, why ball-bearings are used in your bicycle, and why you tend to fall forward when the bus stops suddenly.

You even learn something of how steam, petrol and jet engines work!

A Ladybird Junior Science Book

LEVERS, PULLEYS
and ENGINES

by F. E. NEWING, B.Sc.
and RICHARD BOWOOD

with illustrations by
J. H. WINGFIELD

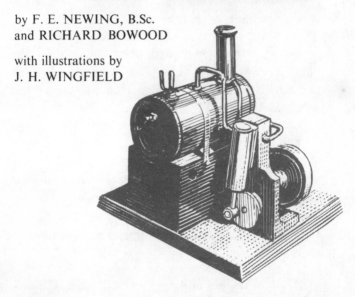

Publishers: Ladybird Books Ltd . Loughborough
© Ladybird Books Ltd (formerly Wills & Hepworth Ltd) 1963
Printed in England

The simplest of Machines

The boy in the picture is lifting a heavy log. It is so heavy that he can only just pick it up. His sister is lifting a similar log quite easily, with a pole resting on a stone. She is using a *machine*. A machine is the scientific word for any device which makes work easier to do.

The girl is using a *lever*, a very simple machine. She is pressing down on the long end, and the short end is pressing upwards against the weight of the log.

Use a lever yourself and observe carefully what happens. Any stout stick or piece of wood will do, or you can do the experiment on the table with a ruler and a few books.

Put the *pivot* on which the lever rests at different distances from the object you are lifting. What do you notice? You will find out that the nearer the pivot is to the object, the less effort is needed at the long end. But when the pivot is close to the object you have to press the long arm of the lever a long way to raise the object a short way.

The boy and girl in the picture both lifted their logs the same distance, but the girl, using much less effort through a longer distance, did the job easily. The boy has had to use a large effort through a short distance. So the *machine* does not give us something for nothing; it just makes the work easier to do.

4

7214 0121 X

Levers of all kinds

The lever is a machine which we use in countless ways. The boy in the picture is digging, and his spade is a lever, because he pulls on the top of the handle to break the earth. The longer the handle the easier it will be.

The girl is looking for levers on her bicycle. As she follows the back brake she finds three: under the handle-bar, at the bottom to take the pull round the corner, and under the pedal leading to the brake blocks. Try putting on a brake by pulling the brake rod with your hand; that will show you how necessary the lever is. Other levers are the pedal cranks, the gear-wheel, the three-speed gear-lever, and, when she mends a puncture, she uses a tyre-lever.

Levers are used everywhere. Think of the signalman in a signal box. His levers are very long, because they work signals and points which are heavy and often a long distance away.

Here are some kinds of levers which make work easier: scissors, nutcrackers, pliers, and fire-tongs; a tin-opener, and a poker to lift the coal in the fire; a coin for

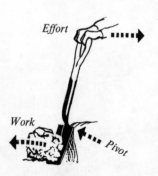

opening a tin; a door latch, like that on a shed door, a lock and key, an electric light switch, a spanner, and many other tools. See if you can find some more. Remember, a lever has three things—the point where you push or pull, the point where it pivots, and the point where the work is done.

6

Science and the See-Saw

A small person on a see-saw can balance a heavier person if they sit in the right places. You will find that to get a balance the heavier person must sit nearer the pivot, or turning point. The heavier one of them is, the nearer he must sit to the pivot. Is there a link between the weights and the distances from the pivot?

You can find out by doing an experiment. Stick a round pencil on a matchbox with a dab of plasticine and carefully balance a long ruler across the pencil.

Put one coin near one end of the ruler and carefully slide two similar coins, one on top of the other, along the other end until the ruler is balanced. Now measure carefully the distances from the centre of the coins to the pivot. You will find that the single coin is *twice as far* from the pivot as the two coins are.

Repeat the experiment, first with the single coin slightly nearer to the pivot, and then nearer still. Each time you must move the other two coins nearer to the

centre. Write down the distances and compare them. You will find that the distance of the two coins from the centre is *always* half the distance of the single coin from the centre.

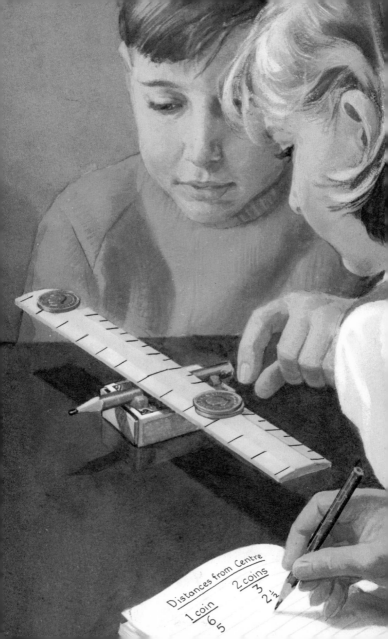

Distances from Centre

1 coin	2 coins
6	3
5	2½

A pair of Scales

A see-saw is a lever, and so is a pair of scales—which the scientist calls a *balance*. Most balances are levers with equal arms—the weights put on them are at equal distances from the pivot. A pound weight on one side will balance a pound of apples on the other side.

You can make a simple balance with a cork, a long knitting needle, and a couple of pins. Cut two pieces out of the cork, as shown in the picture, and push the knitting-needle through so that it balances. The two pins are pushed through the cork near the ends, and the points form the pivot.

Cut two squares of thin card exactly the same size and turn up the corners to make pans. These are hung from the ends of the knitting-needle with cotton at the same distances from the middle. Put two tumblers close together, upside down, and balance the cork between them on the points of the pins. If one pan is higher than the other, put a few grains of sand, or tiny pieces of paper, to make them hang level.

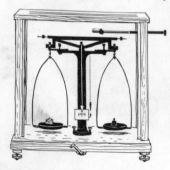

You will not have any weights small enough to use with this balance, but you can weigh small things like pins, matches, or feathers against grains of rice. Instead of ounces, our unit of weight is a grain of rice. A scientist's balance, in its glass case, can accurately weigh articles as light as a single hair.

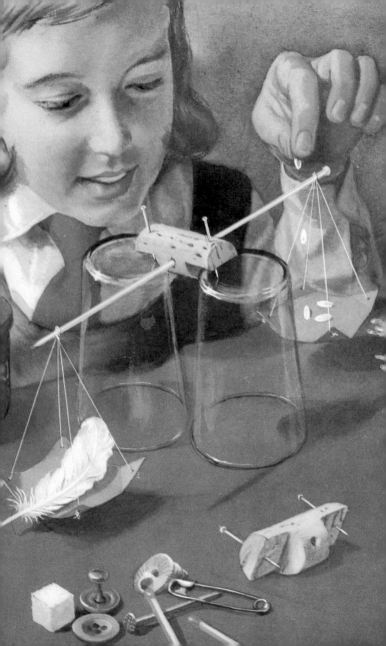

Making it easy to move

In the first picture the girl lifted the heavy log with a lever. How could they both move it to the end of the garden? It was too heavy for them to carry, so they tried to drag it, but it was too difficult. Their problem was the same which often faced primitive man, when he wanted to move a log, a boulder, or perhaps a large slab of stone, like those at Stonehenge or the Pyramids.

They used rollers. If the boy and girl raised their log and slipped round logs underneath it they could roll it along quite easily. Why couldn't they drag it easily? The answer is—*friction*.

The rough surface of the log pressing against the rough surface of the ground hindered the movement. If the log had been smooth and polished, and the ground a sheet of ice, it would have moved easily. When two things rub against each other we say there is *friction*. If they do not touch in so many places the friction is reduced. When rollers are put under a log, it moves by rolling instead of sliding, and the friction is greatly reduced.

Put a pile of books on a table with a table-cloth, and it is difficult to slide them along. Put two or three round pencils under the bottom book and you can roll the pile of books easily. The lever and the roller are machines which make it easy to move things.

12

Ball-Bearings

The roller, a machine for overcoming friction, has been improved to its most perfect form, the *ball-bearing*. This is a perfectly smooth ball of hard steel. It is used in many of the moving parts of machinery to reduce friction as much as possible.

You can see how much a rolling ball can reduce friction by another experiment with the pile of books. Put the books on a tray and try to slide it. Now put half a dozen glass marbles under the tray, and you will find that you can move the pile with your little finger.

In machinery, such as a bicycle or roller-skates, the ball-bearings are contained in what is called a *ball-race*, which you can see in the little sketch. You can make a ball-race with marbles as ball-bearings.

Put the marbles inside the edge of a tin lid. Fit another lid to keep them in position. Put this on the floor and stand on it with one foot. You will be able to spin round very easily—*so easily that you should be very careful not to lose your balance.*

Ball-bearings are mostly used where there is a wheel turning on an axle. You can see where ball-bearings are used on a bicycle—on the axles of the wheels, on the pedal crank, in the pedals themselves, and on the steering column. These are all places where there would be friction through one piece of steel rubbing on another.

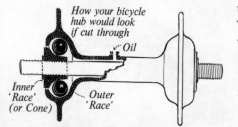

How your bicycle hub would look if cut through

Oil

Inner 'Race' (or Cone)

Outer 'Race'

MAGNETS, BULBS & BATTERIES

LIGHT, MIRRORS AND LENSES

Going and stopping

Have you ever noticed how much better your bicycle runs when you have oiled it? When it has not been oiled you have to pedal harder, because you use more effort to overcome the friction between the moving parts. When these are oiled they slide easily over each other.

If you oil your bicycle properly you will notice that you are putting oil in all the places where there are ball-bearings, and in all other places where metal rubs on metal.

Not only must your bicycle go well; it must slow down and stop well, too. For this friction is necessary. Do you see how? The answer is, of course, the brakes. The brake blocks are made of special material to cause as much friction as possible when they are pressed firmly against the rims of the wheels. When you do this it is the friction which stops the wheels turning.

Pedals and handlebar grips are made so that your

feet and hands will not slip. If there were no friction between the tyres and the road your bicycle would not move at all, the wheels would just spin round. That is why tyres have a tread on them, to grip the road and to prevent you skidding on corners. If you ride with smooth tyres there is less friction, and you might easily skid on a wet road.

A model Crane

To make a model crane like the one in the picture you need a block of wood about two-and-a-half inches thick for the base, two strips about ten inches long for the jib, three empty cotton reels, two wooden skewers, and some nails and thread. The base should be a little wider than the cotton reels.

Make two holes in each strip, one three inches from one end and one half-an-inch from the other. The holes must be big enough to take the skewers.

Fix a cotton reel on each skewer. On one you need about half-an-inch of the skewer sticking out each side; on the other, you need half-an-inch one side and two-and-a-half inches on the other, for the crank-handle. Glue the skewers firmly into the reels.

Nail one of the strips of wood on to the base as in the picture, and put the half-an-inch ends of the skewers in the holes, with the crank-handle at the lower end. Make sure they turn freely in the strip. Now put the other strip in position, with the skewers through the holes, and nail it to the block.

Put a short tin-tack in the top of each jib, and tie thread from each one to the nails in the back of the block. Tack a short strip of wood across the end of the third reel and put a nail in the end to make the handle. Put glue on the long skewer-end and push this reel on to it.

Wind plenty of thread on to the lower reel, take it over the reel at the top and fix a hook, made of soft wire, to the end. Be sure to make the hook heavy enough.

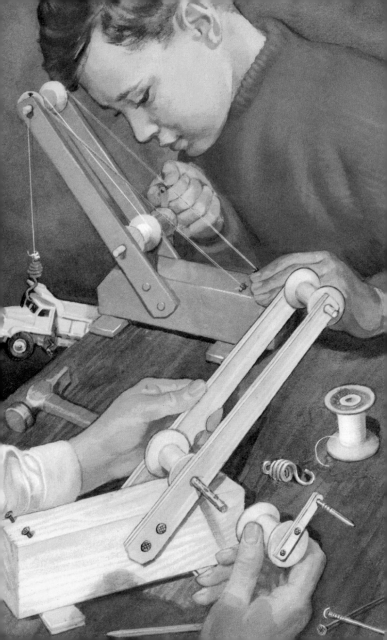

Pulleys

The crane you made is, of course, a *machine*, because it makes work easier. It is easy to turn the handle, but you are not getting 'something for nothing'; you have to do a lot of turning to lift the weight a short distance.

A crane makes it easier to lift a load in another way, too. Because the pulley is at the end of the *jib* and the rope passes over it, the pull is made downwards, which is easier than straight upwards.

The boy and girl in the picture are both lifting a bucket full of earth. The girl finds it difficult, but the boy is using a pulley tied to a beam and is lifting the bucket with the rope passing over the pulley. He has to exert the same pull as his sister, but he finds it much easier to pull *down* on the rope than she does to lift the bucket *up* by the handle.

Single pulleys are very often used to make lifting easier by changing the direction of the pull. They are used in real cranes, and you sometimes see them over loft doors, for hauling up heavy loads. They are used on clothes-drying racks in the kitchen, and sometimes for clothes-lines in the garden.

Pulleys have always been used in sailing ships for hauling up sails. In modern ships they use pulleys on the derricks, or cranes, to load and unload cargo from the ships' holds.

More than one Pulley

You have just found that a single pulley provides a more convenient way to lift a load. If, however, you use *two* pulleys, not only is it more convenient, but it is *easier* as well.

You need two large cotton reels with *deep sides* and two pieces of thick wire which bends easily, each about a foot long. Put them through the cotton reels and bend them as in the picture, making a hook for each reel.

Fix one of the reels to the top of a doorway, or to a beam, with a strong hook or nail. Tie one end of a length of string to another nail or hook on the top of the doorway or on the beam, and thread it round the reels, as you see in the picture. Hang a weight on the lower pulley.

When you pull you will find that the pull you need is very much less than the weight on the hook; the pull is, in fact, about half the weight you lift. But you are still not getting 'something for nothing'; for every foot the weight is raised you have to pull two feet of string through the pulleys.

You can use any number of pulleys, and the more you use the easier the work. The girl is using four pulleys. She only uses a pull of about a quarter the weight she lifts. But for every foot the weight is lifted she has to pull four feet of string through the pulleys.

Cog-Wheels

A clock or a watch contains a number of *cog-wheels*, wheels with teeth cut round the rims, which engage each other. The cog-wheels are of different sizes and are so arranged that the hands they drive turn at different speeds. The big hand goes right round once an hour, the small hand goes right round in twelve hours.

If you have not got any cog-wheels to experiment with you can make some. Get two round boxes, like cheese boxes, of different sizes. Cut strips of strong corrugated cardboard the same width as the edge of the boxes, and glue them firmly round the edges. Pierce holes in the *exact* centres and fix them to a board with long pins, or nails, so that the wheels turn freely and the 'teeth' engage with each other.

. Count the teeth on the two cog-wheels and make a note of the numbers, and make a chalk mark on each wheel where the teeth are engaged. Turn the small wheel completely round once. Count the number of teeth that the big wheel has turned.

You will find, of course, that it is the same number of teeth as there are on the small wheel. For every once that the large wheel turns round, the small wheel will

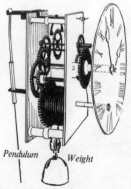

Pendulum   Weight

have turned several times, according to the difference in the number of teeth. You will also notice that the cog-wheels turn in different directions. This is useful for reversing a machine.

Add a third cog-wheel to the other two and do the experiment again. Notice what happens to the speeds and to the directions of turning.

Cogs and Gears

Cog-wheels play a very important part in many kinds of machinery. Their purpose is to make different parts of the machine move at different speeds or in different directions. When you pull a lever on a clockwork engine to make it reverse, you engage other cog-wheels in the motor. When you change gear in a motor car, you change the arrangement of the cog-wheels in the gear-box.

Cog-wheels do not always have to be touching so that the teeth are engaged; they can be joined by a chain which fits over the teeth. The effect is just the same as when the cog-wheels are engaged as regards the speed of the two wheels, but there is one important difference. *With a chain the cog-wheels turn the same way.*

A familiar use of a chain with cog-wheels is on a bicycle. Turn your bicycle upside down and see how the large cog, or *gear-wheel*, on the pedals drives the small gear-wheel on the back wheel by means of the chain. Stick a piece of paper on the tyre, and count how many times the back wheel goes round for one turn of the pedals. If you have a three-speed, change the gear and see how many times the wheel turns then.

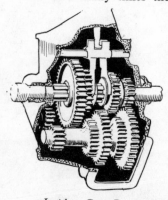

You can push a bicycle along by hand very easily, but when you are riding you have to push much harder on the pedals. It seems as if the bicycle is a machine which makes work *harder*; but remember, this hard work is the price we pay for moving faster.

Inside a Gear Box

26

Tricks with motion

Put an old playing card over the top of an empty tumbler and then put a penny on the card. Flick a corner of the card sharply—and it will fly away. But the penny will stay, and drop into the tumbler. Why?

Another version of the same trick (which you had better not try) is sometimes done in the theatre. A tablecloth is suddenly jerked off a table and the plates, knives and forks and everything stays on the table. Why is this?

Here are some more "Whys". Why do people standing in a bus all jerk backwards if it starts suddenly? Why does the soldier in the picture fall towards the front when the trolley is stopped suddenly? Why, if a horse stops suddenly at a fence, does the rider sometimes go over the horse's head?

The answer to all these questions is one word—*inertia*. Three hundred years ago the great English scientist Sir Isaac Newton defined *inertia*. Put simply, what he said was: "Things which are not moving do not start moving by themselves. Things which are moving do not stop by themselves."

Think about that. The penny was not moving. You flicked the card and that moved, but the penny stayed.

The soldier and the truck were moving together. The truck was stopped, but the inertia of the soldier carried him on, so he fell over, in the direction in which he was moving.

28

Why did the Apple fall?

There is a story that Sir Isaac Newton was once sitting under a tree when an apple fell on his head. If that happened to you, you would probably laugh and eat the apple. But Newton was a scientist, so he asked himself a question—"Why did the apple fall?" You might think that a silly question; everyone knows things fall. Yes, but *why*?

Newton puzzled about that apple, and came to the conclusion that it fell because the earth attracted it. This attraction is known as *gravity*.

The attraction of the earth holds us and everything else on to it. It is rather like the attraction of a magnet for a nail. If you jump upwards it is the attraction of the earth which pulls you down again.

Here are two experiments which show how gravity affects the behaviour of falling objects. Drop a cricket ball and a marble from the same height at the same time. They both hit the floor together. Put a ruler flat on the table, set a penny on the end and another on the table between the ruler and the edge. Flick the ruler so that

it knocks the penny off the table. The coin on the ruler will fall straight down, the other will fall some distance from the table. They started at the same time, and surprisingly, in this case, too, they will both hit the floor at the same time, even though one travelled through a greater distance.

The Pendulum

If you are lucky enough to go to the Science Museum in London, turn left inside the main entrance and watch the famous *pendulum*. A large metal ball hangs on a long wire which is fixed right up at the top of the building. It swings very slowly backwards and forwards. Nearby is a statue of a man holding a pendulum. This is the great Italian scientist Galileo.

Galileo was the first to find out an important fact about the pendulum; if its length is the same it always takes the same time to complete one swing. If it is shortened the swing is faster.

Tie something heavy to a length of string and fix the other end as high as possible so that the weight can swing freely. Start the pendulum, look at the clock and count the number of swings it makes in a minute. Now halve the length of string and time it again. You will find that the shorter pendulum makes more swings in a minute.

Because a pendulum always takes the same time for each swing, Galileo's discovery made it possible to use

the pendulum to make accurate clocks for the first time. Church clocks, grandfather clocks and some wall clocks have a pendulum. Look inside a grandfather clock-case.

Now tie two pendulums, of the same length and with equal weights, to a slack string. Start one of them as the girl has done in the picture, and watch carefully. You will be surprised at the result.

Bending and Bouncing—and the Spring

Hold a rubber ball shoulder high and drop it on a tiled floor or a flagged pavement. Notice how high it bounces. Now drop, from the same height, a glass marble, a ball-bearing and a ball of plasticine. They will all bounce, except the plasticine, and you will probably find that the glass marble and the ball-bearing bounce higher than the rubber ball.

If you bend an india rubber and let go, it springs back. But if you bend a piece of cloth, string or copper wire it does not spring back.

The scientist calls things which spring back or bounce *elastic,* which is how elastic gets its name. The most elastic substances are those which spring back quickest; so, in fact, glass and steel are more elastic than rubber, as you found when you bounced the different balls. Plasticine is not elastic.

When any sort of ball bounces, it is squashed out of shape (much too quickly for you to see) when it hits the ground. It pushes itself off the ground when springing back into shape.

This is the idea used in *springs,* a word which explains itself. A spring is made so that when it is pressed or pulled, it tries to go back to its proper shape. A bow is a spring. Springs are used in all machines and engines, and in watches and clockwork clocks. How many springs have you on your bicycle?

34

Spinning Tops and Gyroscopes

When a top is spinning fast it seems to have a will of its own. Try it and see. Touch a top, which is spinning fast, with your finger. It will move, but it will not go the way you want.

This peculiar behaviour is even easier to see with a bicycle wheel. In the picture the boy has got a wheel spinning while he holds the axle. When he tries to turn the wheel into another direction, he finds that it seems to fight against him. The scientist is always interested in the way things behave, and the spinning top or wheel behaves in an interesting way. The axle, or *axis*, of anything which spins always stays pointing in the same direction.

The earth itself obeys this law. It is always spinning, like a gigantic top, and it spins right round once every twenty-four hours. The *axis*, an imaginary 'axle' through the centre, always points the same way, in the direction of the Pole star.

The *gyroscope*, which is spinning on the table in the picture, is a special kind of top enclosed in a

Earth's Axis

steel ring. It will spin for a long time—*in any position*. This is how the *gyro-compass* works on ships and in aircraft. It spins continuously and so it always stays pointing in the same direction, and can therefore be used as a compass.

Running, Jumping and Throwing

When you walk or run, what do you do? You use your body as a machine. You push back against the ground to walk or run, and it is the *friction* between the ground and your feet which enables you to go forward. Try to run on ice and you will see how necessary this friction is.

The athlete who wants to run as fast as he possibly can wears shoes with sharp spikes, and your football boots have studs to grip the soft ground.

When you jump you push yourself off the ground. If you want to jump a long way you must do two things. You must run as fast as you can before you jump, and you must jump as *high* as you can. Why is this?

The higher you jump, the longer you stay in the air, before the earth's gravitation pulls you down again, and the faster you were moving before you took off, the further you will go in that time. When you practise the long jump, balance a thin rod and jump over it; you will be surprised how much further you will jump.

If you throw a ball straight upwards it doesn't travel

along at all. If you throw it level with the ground it will soon fall. To send a ball a really long way you must aim half way between these two directions. Always, when you throw a ball, or when you throw yourself in a jump, you must have both *speed* and *height* to get distance.

Machines to work Machines

Early man made his work easier by using machines, such as the lever and the wheel. But he always had to provide the *energy* with his own strength and muscles.

Then he had a better idea. He began to use the strength of animals to carry, pull and lift for him. It was much easier to plough the soil with a horse or an ox pulling the plough than by pushing it himself.

One task man always had to do was to grind corn for food, by crushing it on stone or wood. Sometimes animals were used, as when a donkey walked round and round to turn a millstone, sometimes using primitive cog-wheels.

An important step forward was made when man thought of using the energy of flowing or falling water to grind his corn. The flowing water turned blades on a large wheel, and a simple arrangement of cog-wheels turned the grindstone. One machine, the water-wheel, drove another machine, the millstone.

You can make a simple water-wheel. Cut six slots round a cork and slip pieces of strong card into them. Mount the cork on a long darning needle. The cork is mounted on a holder made of bent wire, as shown in the

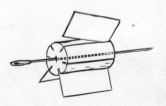

illustration. The card and cork are smeared with vaseline to make them waterproof. Hold it in the sink with a fine trickle of water falling on to the blades and the water-wheel will turn.

The Steam Engine

A water-wheel is driven by moving water. A sailing ship, or a windmill, uses the energy of moving air—the wind. A machine will work, but energy must be fed into it. A sewing machine will not work unless the handle is turned.

In the picture the children have a model steam engine. It works because *heat energy* is put into it. The spirit in the burner boils the water to make steam. The steam is led into the cylinder and pushes the piston. The piston turns the crank which makes the flywheel spin round. The machine works, but only when heat is used to make the steam.

When the steam engine was invented, about two-hundred-and-fifty years ago, man was given a wonderful new machine. It was stronger than a horse and did not get tired, or need sleep. But it had to be fed, with coal instead of oats. Steam engines' power was measured in 'horse power'; an engine which could do the work of ten horses was said to be 'ten horse power'.

The invention of the steam engine was a great event in history. It could drive machines in factories to make things quickly and cheaply. Steam engines were able to pull trains and drive ships, which made it possible to carry people and goods quickly. Soon life was completely changed by the steam engine; this is what the history books call the *Industrial Revolution*.

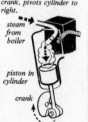

DOWN-STROKE. Steam enters cylinder from boiler through conneeted passages, drives down piston, turns crank, pivots cylinder to right.

steam from boiler

piston in cylinder

crank

UP-STROKE. Piston pushes spent steam out. Cylinder pivots back for more steam, and so on.

The Internal Combustion Engine

The invention of the steam engine brought a great change in our way of life. It was followed by another very important invention—the *internal combustion engine*. This means an engine which burns its fuel *inside* the cylinder. *Internal* means *inside, combustion* means *burning*.

The steam engine burns coal or oil to make steam, which goes into the cylinder to drive the piston. The burning is done *outside* the cylinder. In the internal combustion, or 'inside burning engine', petrol and air are mixed and squirted *inside* the cylinder, where the mixture is exploded by a spark and so drives the piston.

It is this kind of engine which drives motor cars, motor cycles, motor buses and lorries. It put the horse out of work. The new horse was 'fed' with petrol.

The boy in the picture has got a tiny, but a real internal combustion engine to drive the propellor of his model aeroplane. The invention of this kind of engine made the aeroplane possible.

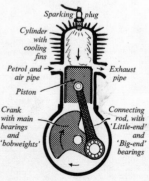

Sparking plug

Cylinder with cooling fins

Petrol and air pipe

Piston

Exhaust pipe

Crank with main bearings and 'bobweights'

Connecting rod, with 'Little-end' and 'Big-end' bearings

The steam engine was much too heavy, however cleverly it was made, to be used in an aeroplane. The internal combustion engine, however, provided just what was needed: a power unit light enough, but sufficiently powerful, to drive a propellor and make an aeroplane fly.

Turbines

Man is always trying to improve the machines he uses, and sometimes he goes back to an old idea, to use it in a new way. When the energy of steam was harnessed to produce power in the steam engine, it occurred to some-one to use steam with a wheel like a water-wheel. It seemed that a wheel with blades in it could be turned by a jet of steam. This led to the invention of the *steam turbine*.

The picture shows a very simple form of steam turbine. The children are using the water-wheel they made earlier. They are holding it in the jet of steam from a kettle, with the jet pointing *away* from them. The energy of the jet of steam is being used to drive the wheel.

A real steam turbine looks very different, of course. It has hundreds of blades set on a long shaft or axle, and it is completely enclosed in a special casing. Turbines provide a smooth and powerful drive. They are used in ships, and they also drive the *generators* that make electricity in power stations.

In the *gas turbine* the blades are turned by jets of hot gases produced by burning special fuels. Another kind of turbine is driven by water.

Where there is a high waterfall, or where rivers or lakes can be dammed to make one, the energy of the falling water is used to drive huge turbines, which drive generators to make elec-tricity. These *hydro-electric* power stations are being built all over the world, usually in mountainous country.

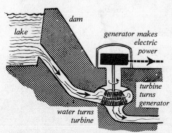

lake

dam

generator makes electric power

turbine turns generator

water turns turbine

46

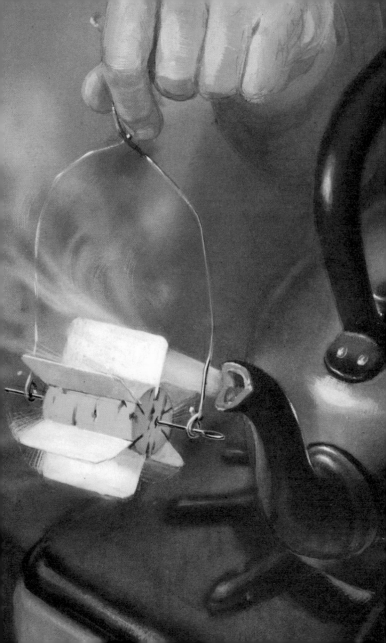

Electric Motors and Jet Engines

One of the ways we use electricity is to feed it into an *electric motor*. The electrical energy drives the motor and provides power we can use. This power can be used in many ways; for working an electric razor, a vacuum-cleaner or even an express train.

Sometimes the electricity comes from the *generators* in a power station, as when a vacuum-cleaner is plugged into a power-point in a room, or when a train runs on an electrified rail. A motor car carries its own generator (called a dynamo) which provides all the electricity the car needs. Electricity can also come from a *battery*, which conveniently stores electrical energy.

To-day we are in what is sometimes called the 'Jet Age'—from the invention of the *jet engine*. Aeroplanes driven by jet engines can fly very much faster than those with propellers driven by piston engines. Very simply we can say that the jet engine burns a mixture of paraffin and air to form a very hot gas at high pressure. This high pressure thrusts the engine *forward* while the exhaust gas rushes out of the back in a *jet*.

You can do an experiment which shows, in a simple way, how a jet engine works. Blow up a balloon and let it go. The air pressure inside the balloon thrusts forward against the rubber, but has nothing to thrust against at the back because the neck of the balloon is open. So the balloon is driven forward. In the picture the children are using a balloon to make a jet-propelled boat.

Air and fuel in

Continuous explosion pushes plane forward

Jet of exhaust gas

Space Rockets and The Atom

The jet cannot fly in outer space because there is no air for it to burn with the paraffin. So to travel up through the atmosphere and into space another form of power had to be found. The answer was the *rocket*.

The rocket works in much the same way as the jet engine; as it is thrust forward it throws out hot gases at the back. But it contains everything it needs for burning, taking its air, or oxygen, with it. The space rocket is a much larger and immensely more complicated version of the rockets we watch on Guy Fawkes night. It is the rocket motor which man is using to explore the mysteries of space.

Another wonder of our age is *atomic energy*. Scientists are discovering how to obtain and use an entirely new, and staggeringly powerful, form of energy. The atom is incredibly tiny; many millions of atoms would go in the point of a pin. Yet the energy which can be released from atoms is infinitely greater than anything man has ever thought of.

Man began by chipping flints to make tools. Then he invented the lever and the wheel. Since the invention of the steam engine tremendous progress has been made in making machines to make work easier. But even in the most complicated modern machines the lever and the wheel are essential parts.

Here is a list of the things you
will need for the experiments in
this book. You will probably
have most of them.

A ruler
Some books
Some round pencils
A match-box
Plasticine - a few pieces
Some coins
Some pins
A knitting-needle
A darning-needle
Some corks
Two tumblers
A reel of cotton
Some grains of rice